FENCE IT

Dek Messecar
Series Consultant Editor: Bob Tattersall

CONTENTS

COLLINS

Introduction

The concept of boundaries is as old as man himself, and the idea of creating them must have occurred almost as far back. The oldest man-made boundary is probably the dry-stone wall, which is still made in exactly the same way today.

Modern fences and walls provide much more than basic privacy and protection. The right boundary treatment can add character and value to your house and help you to make the most of your garden.

It is important that the style of wall or fence you choose should complement your house and be in keeping with others in the locality. This is usually a more important consideration at the front of the house. The face your house presents to the world may dictate the style of wall or fence you choose, as planning authorities and your neighbours' approval may be required. You should consult your local planning regulations at an early stage.

Gardens, especially, benefit from the tasteful use of low and high walls and screens to create interesting spaces, block unsightly views and make features of good

Above *A wooden fence with trellis attached marks the edge of this garden; climbing roses will soon disguise the fence. A dry-stone wall has been used to form a raised bed, adding further interest to a regular-shaped plot.*

Above left *Cottage-style picket fencing is an attractive addition to this country house and gives it a degree of protection from passing traffic.*

Left *Clematis Montana has been allowed to scramble over white-painted trellis, forming an attractive screen.*

ones. As well as protecting plants from the worst ravages of wind and frost, walls and fences are useful for supporting them and so become part of the garden.

In general, fences are easier and cheaper to build than walls but require more frequent maintenance and do not last as long. However, as boundaries are usually permanent, it pays to spend the time and effort required to produce the best results.

The most important stages are planning and preparation. Even the modern systems of fencing must be adapted to your particular situation. Careful measuring and planning will save time and effort during construction. It is a good idea to visit your local supplier to see the many products available and to collect some catalogues. An accurate drawing of your proposed fence will enable your supplier to advise you about the quantities and cost of the materials required.

The photographs and practical step-by-step pages in this book will show the many effects you can create and the techniques you can use to achieve them.

Above *This red brick wall provides a substantial barrier and is entirely in keeping with the architecture of the house it surrounds.*

Left *This black-painted wrought iron gate is an attractive feature in an otherwise heavy stone wall. The flowering shrub also serves to soften the line and greatly enhances this aspect of the garden.*

FENCES

A formal town house may be best suited by a wrought iron fence. Rural settings tend towards wood – either weathered post and rail for a classical look or, perhaps, picket or trellis for a cottage. While this holds true for older houses, modern houses and suburban areas usually allow more variety in choice of styles.

It is in the garden that you can use fences and screens most creatively. There are many ways of using them to alter the too regular shape of most gardens in the overall effect. On the other hand, you could use some of the many inexpensive, modern fencing products to keep the cost as low as possible, concealing the fence with climbing plants and shrubs.

When selecting a type of fence, consider the various practical results you want and choose fencing that enables you to achieve them. For instance, you may want to keep small children away from a pond or out of reach of the road; to prevent rather larger children from using your property as a shortcut or playground; to keep others' pets out and your own in; or to provide shade or allow sunlight to pass through, while giving protection against the wind.

The question of security and privacy is also important. While a high fence may protect your house from prying eyes, be careful not to create any spaces where someone breaking in will be screened from the view of neighbours or passers-by. You can design your fence with a balance between security and privacy by varying the height at appropriate places. An effective way of doing this is to erect a fence of constant height and add trellis to the top where necessary. Climbing plants can be used to complete the screen effect.

For shelter from the wind the best protection is given by fences that allow some air to pass through. Their effect is to slow the air down: fences which obstruct the air completely force it to spill over the top and create turbulence which can be as annoying as the wind itself.

Above *This white plastic fence has been used to mark the boundary without detracting from the floral display.*

Right *Tall picket fence has been erected in an irregular line to help the general apperance of the neighbourhood. With clever planting this will also give the garden a more interesting shape.*

Left *Metal post and chain are sufficient to mark the boundary.*

Below *This wrought iron fencing on top of a low wall is in keeping with the town house. If you are getting a contractor to repair or replace such a railing, make sure you get the same pattern.*

Types of Fence

Having considered the appearance and purpose of your fence, give some thought to the practical side of erecting and maintaining it. Some fences will last for many years with no maintenance at all, while others will require attention as often as twice yearly. Also bear in mind that although modern products have made fencing much easier there is still quite a lot of labour in digging post holes, mixing concrete, cutting to size, and so on. Do not underestimate the time and effort needed for a good result.

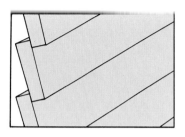

The boards can be featheredge or waney edge, slightly overlapping each other.

Wooden fences

Wood is strong, easy to work with hand tools and has an attractive, natural appearance whether left to weather or painted. It is also inexpensive and widely available.

The main disadvantage wood has in fencing is that it needs protection against deterioration and rot. These should be considered as separate problems. Rot is the decay that occurs when wood is kept moist and away from sunlight, as happens when posts are sunk into the earth. The open grain on the end of the post readily soaks up water and because there is no ventilation stays permanently saturated. Untreated softwood posts may last only a year or two below ground.

Modern fenceposts are made of softwood which has been pressure or vacuum treated with a long-lasting fungicide which greatly extends its life. They are superior to those dipped in creosote, but both types need annual treatment with a preservative.

Deterioration is the distortion and splitting that can be caused when wood is alternately soaked by rain and dried by wind and sun. End grain is especially vulnerable.

How severely it is affected depends on how the fence is built and the treatment it receives. Every effort must be made to slow the passage of water and water vapour through the wood. This moderates the distortion.

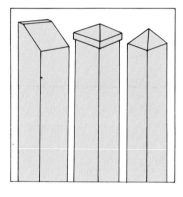

Shaping the tops of posts will ensure that rain water does not stand on them, but caps on post tops are much better. The tops are then protected both from the rain and from the drying effect of wind and sun, which can cause splitting. Capping-rails over panels serve the same purpose.

The horizontal *close-boarded fence* is one of the simplest types. It has horizontal boards nailed to posts. The boards are butt-joined (end-to-end) at every other post.

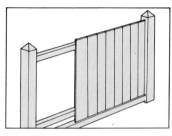

Vertical close-board fences have rails joined to the posts, to which vertical boards similar to the horizontal type are nailed.

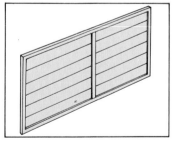

Both of these types of fence can be bought ready-made in the form of panels. These have a simple frame to which the boards have been nailed and are usually available in several heights. The most common length is 1.8m, although it is easy to cut them to length where necessary.

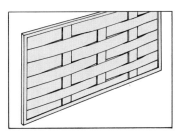

The *woven fence-panel* is another that comes ready made. It has vertical battens around which the thin boards are bent, giving a basket-weave effect.

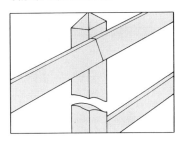

Post and rail fence has rails nailed to one or both sides of the posts or fixed into mortises in the posts. Both are sturdy fences which use less timber than the panel types, though the rails are much thicker and the posts must be securely set as there is no bracing to hold the fence rigid.

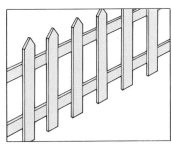

The *picket (or palisade) fence* is similar to the post and rail

with the addition of vertical palings fixed to the rails. The tops of the palings are shaped, both for appearance and to ensure that water will run off.

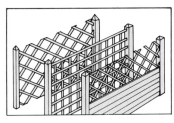

There are many designs of *trellis* available in panels. The more substantial ones can be used as fence panels, either as a full-height fence or above a wall or fence.

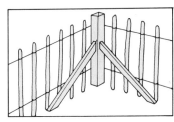

Palings are chestnut stakes held together with twisted wire in place of rails. They are sold in rolls ready to be stretched between posts. This means that any posts not in a straight line will need bracing, as the wire must be taut to make a sound fence.

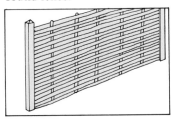

Wattle and *hurdle* are the names given to fence panels

made of woven willow or hazel rods. Thicker vertical stakes hold them together and protrude from the bottom to pierce the ground to give a little additional support.

Concrete fences

Precast concrete is the least expensive and most durable fencing material. While not the most attractive, it can be concealed by plants and shrubs.

Alternatively, use concrete for the most vulnerable parts of the fence (those on or below ground level) and other materials for the more conspicuous parts.

The concrete fence parts most frequently used are spurs, posts and gravel boards. It is not possible to cut or drill precast concrete, so it is important to buy the type suitable for your fence.

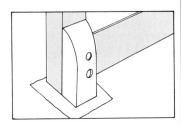

Spurs are short lengths of posts used to support and repair wooden posts. They are set in concrete below ground, allowing the wooden posts to remain above. This is useful where wooden posts have rotted below ground, but are still in good condition above. The spurs have holes through which fixings can be made to the wood.

Precast concrete fence posts

are made in several types, each with the appropriate corner post available. Braces are also made and some posts have notches to receive them.

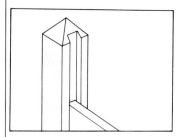

Some are made with grooves down the sides to hold concrete or ready made wooden panels.

Concrete panels are usually arranged horizontally and are held in the grooves. They can have various decorative surfaces to simulate stone or wooden slats or louvres.

Most of the ready-made wooden fence panels can be used with the posts, but be sure the panels you choose are suitable for the grooves in your posts. The safest way is to buy all the parts from the same supplier.

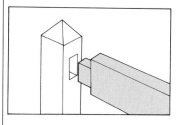

Other posts have mortise holes ready for wooden rails, or notches for fixing close-board wooden panels to the front of them. The notched posts usually have chamfered tops which are completely

hidden behind the panels, making it easy to hide the posts with plants.

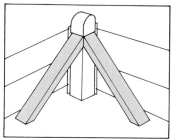

Concrete posts are made for use with all the steel wire fences. Buy the posts made for the particular type of fence you want and the fixing holes will be in the right places. There must be notches in the sides for braces where fencing is to be stretched between posts.

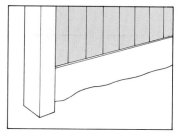

Concrete gravel boards are used to fill the space left below the panels. By sinking where necessary, they take up the unevenness of the ground. Concrete is the best material for this because it is durable and discourages animals from digging under the fence.

Metal fences
Wrought iron fences and railings are a familiar sight but, even though modern versions are made of steel, they tend to be expensive. It is

usually necessary to have them made to measure and professionally installed. They require cutting and welding and are fitted into holes in stone or concrete kerbs with molten lead.

However, there are some inexpensive steel fencing kits that make lightweight fences for decorative borders or to fix along the top of a wall. Erecting them requires only some sawing and drilling.

A main consideration is that whereas wrought iron is very resistant to rusting, steel is not. So you will need to treat and paint the finished fence and repaint it regularly to keep it in good condition. This can be quite time-consuming with the more ornate designs.

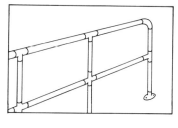

A modern-looking railing can be made using *galvanised water pipe* as the rails. There are precast concrete posts available with holes to receive the pipes or purpose-made galvanised posts and fittings to bolt together. They are very strong and durable and look good when painted.

Steel wire, either galvanised or plastic-coated, is the basis for several types of fence. Because it needs to be stretched taut, the posts must be securely set. Corner and end posts will need to be braced.

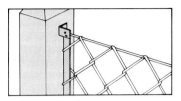

Chain-link fencing is made of woven wire, either galvanised or plastic-coated, and is sold in rolls. It is held in stretcher bars on each post and reinforced with wires that run between the posts.

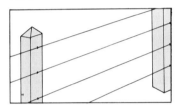

Simple *post-and-wire fencing* has galvanised steel wire stretched taut between the posts.

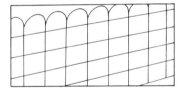

Welded mesh is sold in rolls in various decorative patterns or occasionally in rigid panels. Some versions have wires protruding at the bottom for driving into the ground.

Plastic fencing

Plastic is used as a fencing material in a decorative form imitating welded steel wire mesh or as a version of the post-and-rail or picket fence. Although expensive, plastic has the advantage that the colour runs right through the material, so painting and maintenance are completely eliminated.

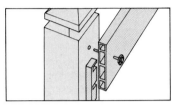

The parts are hollow and can be cut to size with woodworking tools. The posts are set in concrete and the rails are fastened on with special bolts. Post caps and end covers snap together. Alternatively, plastic chains can be draped between posts.

Other fencing products

In addition to the posts, rails, and panels that make up a fence there are many products available to reduce the work of constructing or repairing one.

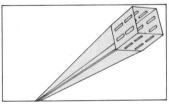

One of the most useful is the metal socket for 75mm and 100mm square wooden posts. There are drainage holes in the bottom of the sockets so that water runs away and the end grain of the post is ventilated.

Posts that are too tight may need to be tapered to fit; loose ones can have wedges hammered in. Some sockets have a nut and bolt to ensure a tight fit.

The sockets may have spikes on the bottom for driving into firm ground, though they are better set in concrete plugs in normal post holes. Concrete protects steel quite effectively so the spikes last much longer than if just in earth.

Driving your posts into the ground instead of digging post holes can be more difficult in the end because, if you are using ready-made panels, the posts need to be positioned accurately. Any rock, root or rubble below ground sends the post out of line and the more you try to straighten it the looser the spike becomes. However, where the distance between posts is not too critical and the ground is firm and clear of obstructions, you can drive the sockets in using a dolly (a short length of post with a metal top) and a sledge hammer. This does not provide as strong or as permanent a fixing as setting in concrete but it is suitable for a lightweight fence or for a temporary one – the posts are easily removed.

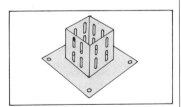

There are also sockets with tabs on the bottom instead of spikes. These are for bolting down to patios or decking. They provide the best means of erecting posts where the fence must cross paved areas, or to fix on top of a wall.

Building Fences

The first step with all fences is to plan the layout. This should be done even before deciding the type of fence to buy. Knowing all the obstructions and slopes you will encounter and where the posts will be sited will make it possible to measure accurately and save a lot of time and effort later.

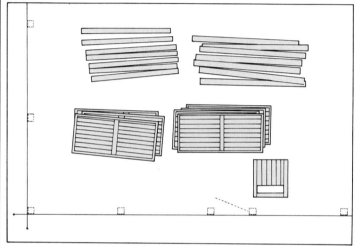

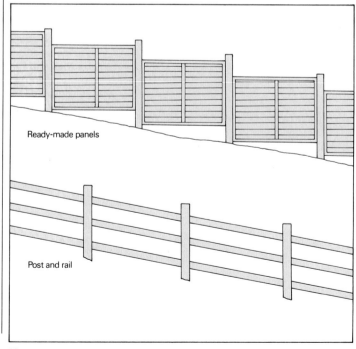

Ready-made panels

Post and rail

Peg a string following the line of the inside or outside of the posts, clearing away long grass and obstructions.

Posts at corners and gates should be marked first. Then measure the lengths of the runs of fence between them.

A catalogue from your supplier is a useful source of information about the widths of gates available, the lengths of panels and rails and recommended distances between posts.

You will need to take account of any change in ground level and set the height accordingly.

Fence posts should be vertical so, if you have a gradual slope, ready-made square panels will need to be stepped and any gaps beneath filled by gravel boards. If you are using wooden posts the panels will be held in grooves or fixed with metal brackets, so the height of the posts is not critical. They can be put in first and the panels fixed temporarily, to be adjusted later. The tops of the posts can be cut off after the panels have been fixed. Be sure to treat the cut ends with preservative before fixing post caps.

If you are using concrete posts you will need to find the correct heights of each post as you erect them, as you will not be able to cut them afterwards.

Post-and-rail, picket or vertical close-boarded (not ready-made) look best following the slope at a constant height from the ground. In this case the posts will all be similar in length, making it possible to use posts that are already mortised.

Tools

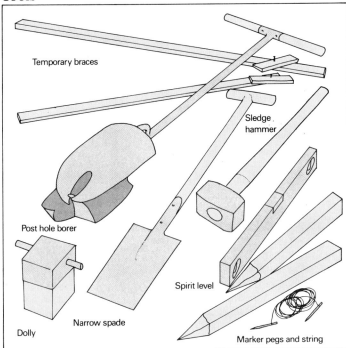

Temporary braces

Sledge hammer

Post hole borer

Spirit level

Dolly

Narrow spade

Marker pegs and string

A *post-hole borer* is a time-saving tool that can be hired inexpensively. It is best to dig all the holes at once to minimise the cost of hiring.

You use it by turning it clockwise into the earth until it is full, and then lifting it out of the hole to empty it.

Where there are stones, rubble or large roots you need to dig out the obstructions as you meet them.

A *narrow spade* is best for digging out the hole without too much disturbance of the soil around the edges. This helps to keep the post firm.

A *spirit level* is necessary to set posts vertically and rails and gates horizontally. Be sure to get the type that works both ways.

A *dolly* is a block of post wood with a solid metal cap and is used for driving in metal post sockets. Suppliers of posts and sockets usually provide with them a dolly of the appropriate size.

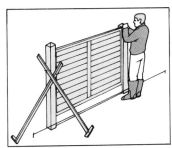

A *pair of temporary braces* are necessary to hold posts straight before concreting. Use a single nail to fix a length of batten to

a stake and clench the nail over. Then drive a nail just through the other end of the batten. Make two for each post.

Erecting posts

Wooden posts can be set into metal post sockets that have been set in concrete (the best method), or the sockets can be driven into the ground. Although the sockets may seem an extra expense you will be buying shorter posts, making the difference negligible.

Alternatively, you can set the posts directly into the holes and secure them either with hard core and earth rammed down, or with concrete (see page 20) poured around them. However, these methods require quite a depth to hold the post securely, and they encourage rotting. It is advisable to soak the bottom of the posts (even pre-treated ones) in preservative for a day or so before use.

The depth of your post holes will depend on the height of the fence and the firmness of the ground. As a guide, about one third of the post should be below ground.

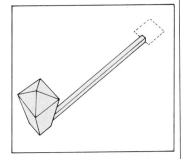

If you are using ready made panels (or rails already cut to

length), cut a timber batten exactly the right length to set the distance between the posts. Allow for grooves in mortises in the posts if necessary.

Dig the post holes about 250mm square, or use a post-hole borer. Put some hard core (broken bricks or stones) into the bottom of the hole and ram it down firmly.

Using the string as a guide, set the first post in position and brace it with battens.

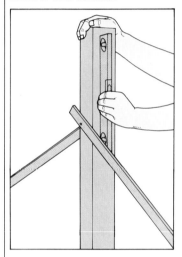

Drive the stake into the ground an appropriate distance from the post. Hold a spirit level against the post to ensure it is vertical and tap the partially driven nail to fix the batten to the post.

Repeat using a second brace on an adjacent face of the post. It helps to jam some hard core around the socket spike or post to locate it in the hole.

Then fit a panel into the groove or metal bracket (or the rails into the mortises) and place the second post in position.

You can now fix the panel or rails to the posts if you are certain of the height. Use a spirit level on top of the panel to check that it is level. Drive the nails only part of the way in, as you may need to adjust it later.

If you brace the posts well, you can complete the whole fence before securing the posts with concrete. When using ready-made panels or mortised rails, it is important to fix them between the posts as you go.

If you are driving post sockets into the ground, place the dolly in the socket and drive it into the ground until the bottom of the socket is just above ground level. If it tries to twist out of line or lean, keep readjusting

it, if necessary by placing a post in it for leverage.

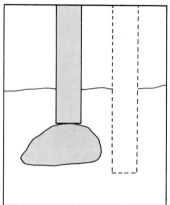

If it strikes a large rock below ground, remove the socket and dig out the obstruction; then try to ram the earth back into the hole to compact it enough to hold the socket next time.

If you are cutting your own rails to length you can site your posts without worrying quite so much about the distance between them. It may be easier to move a socket away from an obstruction.

Setting concrete posts

Concrete posts are set in the same way as wooden ones except that they are always set directly into the post holes and secured with concrete. As with wooden ones, if the distance between posts is critical, they must be braced and have panels or rails fitted between them before the concrete is poured. However, because you cannot cut off the tops afterwards you need to ensure that they are at the correct height as well as vertical. Use a spirit level along a rail or the top of a panel to check.

Fixing panels

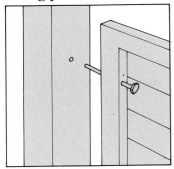

Ready-made fence panels are fixed either by nailing through pre-drilled holes in the frames or by using metal brackets.

Concrete posts should have holes for bolting fixings through.

Fixing mortised rails

For a post-and-rail, picket or vertical close-board fence where the rails are mortised into the posts, you will need to fix the rails into each pair of posts as they are erected.

The mortises should be cut into wooden posts before erecting them. A lot of time and effort is saved by buying posts already mortised.

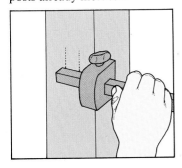

To make your own mortises, first mark each post at the same place for the required

length of rails. Then use a mortise gauge set to the thickness of your rails between the pencil lines.

Remember to mark corner posts on two adjacent faces, intermediate posts on two opposite faces and gate posts on one face only.

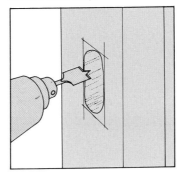

Use a flat bit, of the same width as the mortise, in an electric drill to remove as much waste wood as possible. Use a depth stop set to just over half the thickness of the post, drilling the intermediate posts from each side rather than straight through.

Then use a mortise chisel of the same width and a mallet to clean out the remaining waste up to the marked lines.

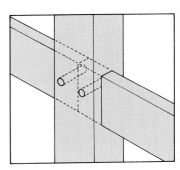

Join the rails at each post so they meet in the middle. It may be necessary to angle the ends where the fence rises and falls on sloping ground. Fix them with nails driven at an angle through the rail into the post. A stronger fixing can be made by drilling two holes through the post and rail and knocking a dowel into each one. Stagger the holes so that they do not follow the grain of the post.

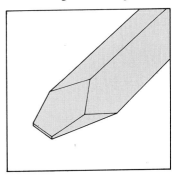

Arris rails for vertical close-board fences are cut to length and then shaped at the ends to fit the mortises.

Face-fixed rails

Where rails are to be fixed on the face of the posts (rather than in between) all the posts should be erected first and concrete allowed to set.

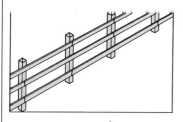

For post-and-rail fences, it is best to join the rails on alternate posts, and to stagger the joins so that each post has at least one unjoined rail. The rails can be nailed or screwed to the posts but as the fixings are quite near the ends of the rails, a pilot hole should be drilled to prevent splitting. A much stronger fixing can be made with galvanized coach bolts.

Fixing gravel boards

Wood or concrete gravel boards are fixed under panel fences to fill the space just above the ground. If you are using concrete posts with grooved sides, the gravel boards must be fitted as you erect the fence. In the case of wooden posts, you can fix them as you go or after the whole fence is up. There are fittings available for fixing both types to wood or concrete posts.

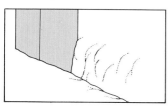

Dig out a groove between the posts to accept the gravel board and insert into the fixings.

Chain-link

All stretched wire fences are erected after posts have been set and the concrete has cured.

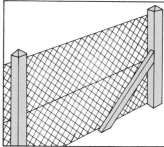

Each length of chain link mesh is held taut by stretcher bars attached by adjusting bolts to braced posts (called straining posts). Along its length it is supported by horizontal wires attached to intermediate posts. There should be a wire at the top and another at the bottom for fences up to 1m high; add a central wire for taller fences.

Thread a stretcher bar through one end of the rolled up mesh, and fix it to the straining post with the bolts provided. Leave as much adjustment as possible on the bolts. Unroll the mesh, keeping it as taut as possible, as far as the next straining post.

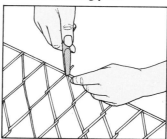

Untwist one of the vertical zigzag wires at the top and

bottom and remove it, separating the length from the roll.

Thread a stretcher bar through the end of the mesh and attach it to the post as before.

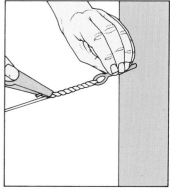

Fasten a length of supporting wire between the eyes of the bolts by twisting the ends.

Tighten the wires and the mesh by doing up the bolts.

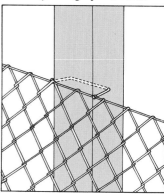

Finally, secure the wires to the intermediate posts with wire ties.

Permanent bracing

Gate posts, straining posts and corner posts used with stretched fencing need to be permanently braced.

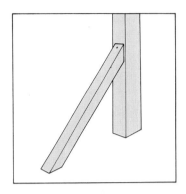

Dig a hole at an appropriate distance from the post and set the brace in it in the same way as for a fence post, making sure that the brace does not interfere with the fence. Concrete posts should have notches with fixing holes for concrete braces. Wooden posts can be braced with concrete braces by cutting a notch and drilling fixing holes in the same way.

To make a wooden brace, cut a length of post about ¾ of the length of the post to be braced. Set this into a hole to the same depth as the post and cut the top end to the appropriate angle and nail to the post.

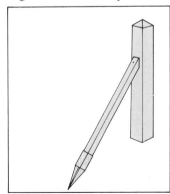

You can also set the wooden brace in a post socket.

Uses of trellis

Trellis can be nailed to the inside face of fence posts either from the ground up as a support for plants, or just along the top. Use vertical strips of trellis on the posts to support the plants between the ground and the bottom of the horizontal trellis.

To add trellis to the top of an existing fence without extra tall posts, nail 50mm x 25mm battens to the sides of the posts to provide the supports.

Expanding diamond-shaped trellis is the most convenient type to use where it is to be fitted between posts, as you can extend it to the length required.

Narrow panels of grid-shaped trellis can be nailed together to make square columns around a plant, to protect it while small and to support it later. Two or more columns can be joined by horizontal trellis at the top to carry climbers over paths.

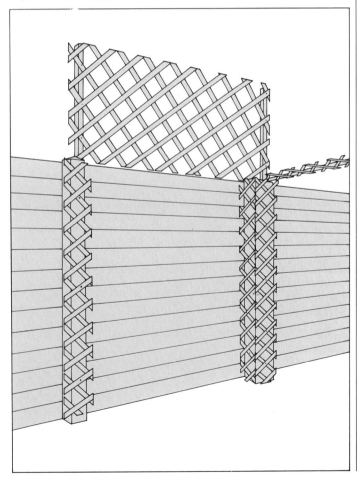

WALLS

Walls give a feeling of permanence to a property. Stone always looks traditional, but there are now many types of brick and block available in both traditional and modern styles.

Walls are more durable and substantial than fences, but are also more expensive and require more effort and skill to build.

It is essential that they should be built on solid, level foundations that are capable of supporting them. Even a small wall can be dangerous if it falls over. While low walls are within the scope of the average home-owner, professional advice should be sought about walls more than 1.5m in height.

Above *Obtain an interesting effect like this by using different colours of brick. In deciding to undertake this type of design, make sure that you like it and that it will not upset your neighbours opposite, as a wall is often for a lifetime and is too expensive to replace.*

Left *Compare the two methods of finishing off the top of a brick wall: the old one has up-ended bricks laid side by side, while the one in the rear has a stone coping.*

Above *A modern stone wall in which mortar has been used. Roses have been planted to help break up the long line.*

A concrete screen wall provides an attractive, practical and long lasting solution.

Materials

Types of bricks

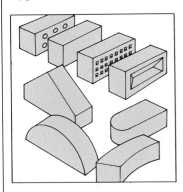

Standard size bricks measure 215mm x 103mm x 65mm and are divided by appearance into common and facing bricks. *Commons* (or *stocks*) are used for walls that will be rendered, or where appearance is not important, although they can create just the right effect if there is other weathered brickwork near. *Facing bricks* have a special finish on one or more face and are more expensive.

Colour and texture vary considerably with traditional bricks. Clay from different areas produces different colours, and texture is influenced by the techniques used in moulding or cutting. Modern bricks are available in an even larger range of colours and textures. As well as the modern architectural styles, there are bricks with antique finishes and some even simulate stone.

Most standard bricks have a pyramid-shaped depression, called a *frog*, in one face to reduce weight and to increase the strength of the mortar bond between courses. Others may have holes or slits for the same purpose.

Specially shaped bricks are also made for many purposes. Some are for copings and others are curved at one end for rounded corners.

Airbricks can be used in place of a standard brick to allow ventilation.

Bricks are graded according to their resistance to water and frost damage and also by their load-bearing capacity. It is unlikely that you will be concerned with loads, but it is important to use bricks that will stand up to the weather. You can use moderately frost-resistant bricks if you incorporate two or three courses of frost-proof ones for the bottom courses and provide good coping protection on top of the wall. Check with your supplier before choosing.

Bricks are given different names according to their position in a wall. If a brick is laid with its length in the direction of the wall, it is called a *stretcher*. If it is laid across the width of the wall, it is a *header*. A *bat* is a brick cut across its width; one cut down its length is called a *closer*.

Types of blocks

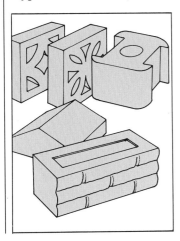

The advantage of blocks is that they are larger (and usually lighter) than bricks, making them easier to lay. Because natural stone is expensive and not readily available, they provide a reasonable alternative with similar appearance.

Simulated stone blocks are made of crushed, reconstituted stone and can look quite realistic. Some are made in several sizes to be used at random, some are one size to be used in the same way as bricks, and some large ones have joint lines in them to look like several courses.

Blocks are laid similarly to bricks: but follow the manufacturer's instructions.

A quite different type of block is the pierced-screen block. These are made in many decorative patterns and are usually laid in stacked bond between pilaster block columns. The pilaster blocks have holes vertically through the centre so they can be reinforced by vertical steel rods from the top of the column through to the bottom.

Tools

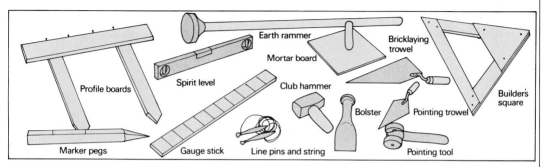

Earth rammer

Bricklaying trowel

Mortar board

Spirit level

Profile boards

Club hammer

Builders square

Bolster

Pointing trowel

Marker pegs

Gauge stick

Line pins and string

Pointing tool

Profile boards with strings stretched between them mark the outline of the foundation trench.

Marker pegs are stakes marked with the depths of the foundation materials.

A spirit level is used to ensure that the wall is plumb and level.

A gauge rod is a wooden batten marked with the height of the courses.

Line pins and string are used to keep the courses level. They are inserted into the mortar at each end of a course with string stretched between them.

A bolster and *club hammer* are used to cut bricks and blocks to size. Mark a line around all four sides and place the brick on sand or grass. Tap the bolster with the hammer to score the lines. Lay the brick frog down, place the bolster on the line and break the brick with one hard blow.

A builder's square is used to keep corners at 90 degrees.

A mortar board or *hawk* is used to hold a small amount of mortar to work with.

A bricklaying trowel is used to cut and shape a quantity of the wet mortar to place under each brick.

The smaller *pointing trowel* is used to point the joints between bricks. A *roller pointing tool* can be used instead of a trowel.

An earth rammer is used to ram down the hardcore in the foundation trench.

You will also need two buckets, two spades and a watering can for mixing concrete.

Types of bond

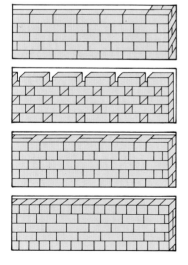

Bricks, blocks and stones are laid in horizontal rows called *courses. Bonds* are the names given to the patterns whose purpose is to tie the wall together.

Stretcher bond is for a wall one brick-width wide. It is called a half-brick wall as it has a bat at the end of every other course. It must be supported with piers at the ends and at 2m intervals.

Open bond is laid with a quarter-brick gap between stretchers.

Flemish bond makes a wall one brick-length (215mm) wide.

Each pair of stretchers are separated from the next by one header.

English garden-wall bond has three pairs of stretcher courses alternating with one of headers.

Other bonds (not illustrated) include *Stack bond*, used for pierced-screen blocks between pilasters, and *Random Bond* which can be used with simulated stone blocks.

Dry stone walls are made by selecting stones to fit well together with occasional stones as headers to bridge the full width of the wall.

Building a Wall

Parts of a wall

Brick, block and stone walls all require three main things: foundations, or *footings*, of a width and depth to support their weight; some means of lateral (sideways) support such as piers, which act rather as fenceposts; and *copings*, which are waterproof cappings to prevent water penetrating the fabric of the wall and causing frost damage.

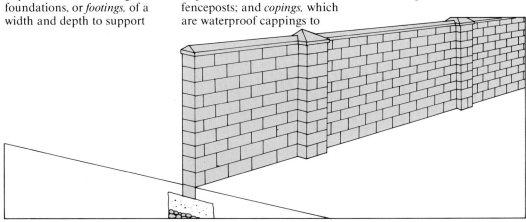

Foundations for walls are called *strip foundations*. They are made by digging trenches of a width and depth to suit the wall and the type of soil. A layer of hard core is rammed down firmly and then covered with a layer of sharp sand or ballast to fill the gaps. Then a layer of concrete is poured up to just below ground level.

Piers are columns built into walls to give support. They are not usually necessary where walls turn corners, but are always used at free ends, such as either side of a gate.

Copings are used on the tops of walls and piers to prevent water penetration. There are many concrete and simulated stone ones available, or weatherproof bricks on edge or roofing tiles can also be used.

Cement mortar and concrete

Cement mortar is used to lay bricks, blocks and stones. You need a smooth, hard area,

preferably next to a wall, on which to mix it. If that is not available a sheet of plywood or something similar will do.

The mix for mortar is one part Portland cement to three parts soft sand with the addition of a plasticiser. This is added to make the mortar smooth and to improve its adhesion to the bricks. It is sold as a liquid and should be added according to the manufacturer's instructions.

Mortar stays fresh for about two hours, so mix it in small amounts as you work.

Remember to use two buckets and shovels for mixing, keeping one of each dry for the cement only.

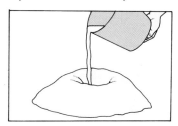

Measure ¾ of a bucket of sand onto the board and ¼ of cement. Keep turning over the pile with the shovel until the sand and cement are fully mixed. Add the plasticiser. Make a crater in the top of the pile and add a little water from the watering can.

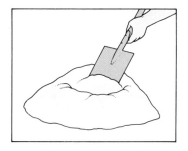

Use the shovel to scoop the rim of the crater into the centre and turn over each shovelful. When the water is mixed, sprinkle a little more on the pile and keep mixing until you have a stiff mixture that holds together and slides cleanly off the shovel.

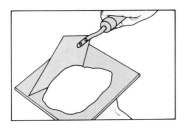

Use a trowel to load the mortar board with a convenient amount.

Leave the remainder in a neat pile on the mixing board and cover with polythene to prevent its drying out.

You cannot revive mortar by adding more water and mixing.

Concrete is a mixture of sharp sand, course aggregate (small stones or gravel) and cement. The dry ingredients are available separately, or they can be purchased dry in bags, requiring only water. Concrete is also available ready-mixed from a truck, to be poured down a chute into the already-prepared foundation site. If the site is not near enough to the truck the mixture has to be carried in wheelbarrows.

Once mixed it must be laid in two hours, so it is advisable to have helpers.

In making foundations for walls it is probably best to use the dry bag variety. The slightly greater cost is offset by having the measuring already done.

You can mix concrete in a cement mixer or, for smaller quantities, on a large mixing board.

When pouring foundations it is important that the concrete slab should be cast all

at once. If you are mixing batches, make sure you have the next one ready soon after each one is poured.

The right mix for foundations and for setting fence posts is one part cement to 2.5 parts sharp sand and 3.5 parts coarse aggregate.

These can be measured by the shovelful, rather than using buckets as with mortar, but remember to keep one shovel dry for the cement.

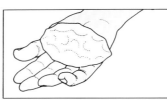

Mix the sand and aggregate together and add the cement, mixing until it is all the same colour. Make a crater in the top and add a little water from the watering can. Keep shovelling the outside of the pile inwards and turning it over. Continue adding water and mixing until it is just moist right through. A squeezed handful should just about hold its shape and be slightly crumbly.

Making strip foundations

Foundations, or footings, should be between two and three times the width of wall they support, including the piers. The depth depends on the height and weight of the wall.

As a guide, a half-brick wall up to 1.2m high would need a 300mm layer of hard core topped by a 150mm layer of

concrete. A full width wall of the same height needs a 300mm layer each of hard core and concrete.

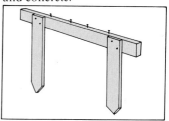

The first step is to make profile boards to set the width of trench. Nail two stakes to a batten and drive nails on the top edge to mark the edges of the trench.

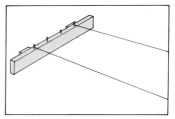

Drive in the profile boards some distance beyond either end of the trench, and stretch strings between the corresponding nail on each.

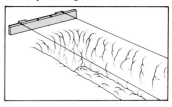

Dig out the turf or topsoil from the area of the trench, and use it somewhere in the garden.

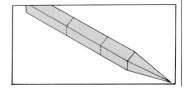

21

Cut enough marker pegs to use one a metre down each edge of the trench. Measure from the tops of all the pegs and mark lines to show the depth of the concrete and hardcore. Leave about 250mm on the bottom of the pegs below the bottom of the hardcore.

The concrete will be laid flush with the tops of the pegs. Drive a peg into the ground at each corner and the others about 1m apart down each side of the trench.

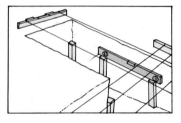

Use a spirit level to keep the tops of the pegs level. The finished foundation should be about 50mm below the level of the turf or level with any adjacent paving. Use a length of straight board to check the level of several pegs at once.

Dig out the trench down to the lower line on the marker pegs. Try not to disturb the soil in the trench bottom. If it is loose, it is better to dig deeper until it is firm.

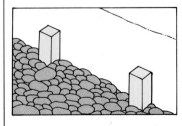

Fill the trench with hard core up to the higher line on the

marker pegs. Use a rammer to pack it down hard, adding more hard core as necessary. It is important to pack it down as firmly as possible. Try moving individual pieces around to fill gaps and level it overall.

The next step is to consolidate the hard core with a layer of sand and gravel (aggregate) to help fill up the spaces.

Use a shovel to throw the sand and gravel over the whole surface of the hard core, using as much as necessary to fill it in. Tamp down the surface to ensure it settles into all the gaps.

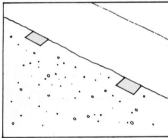

Shovel in the concrete, filling up to the tops of the marker pegs. Use a rake or shovel to push it well into the corners and edges.

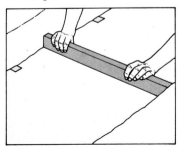

Finally, use a convenient length of timber to level off the concrete to the tops of the pegs.

tamp the surface frequently to make sure air does not remain trapped below.

When you are satisfied that the surface is smooth and level, remove the marker pegs and fill the holes with concrete.

The foundation must be left for three days before building or walking on it. It is best to cover it with polythene sheeting to keep the surface moist during this time. The concrete will take 28 days to cure to full strength.

Laying bricks

Begin by stretching strings along the foundations to mark the lines of the first course of bricks.

Mix up a small batch of mortar to start with, as it is important to lay the first course straight and level. On hot days, keep a bucket of water to dip each brick into before laying. This will prevent the mortar from drying too quickly and spoiling its adhesion to the bricks.

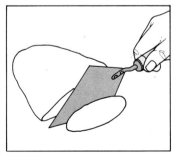

Cut and shape a trowelful of mortar as shown, and place it in position on the end of the first course. Then use the trowel to flatten it to about 18mm thick. The weight of the brick and tapping with the trowel handle will squeeze it to the finished thickness of 10mm.

Place the brick frog upwards on the mortar, being careful to align it with the string guides. Temporarily lay a second brick in the same way a metre or so away from the first and use a straight board and spirit level to make them level with each other. To adjust a brick, tap it with the trowel handle.

Place some mortar in the position next to the first brick. Hold the second brick end upwards and scrape a layer of mortar on to the end. Scrape around the edges to stick the mortar on and to prevent it from falling off.
Place the second brick in position and push it up to the first.

Lay several more bricks in the same way before using the spirit level and adjusting them. Tap down bricks that are too high and remove and add mortar beneath any that are too low.

Remove the temporary brick when you come to it.

When you finish the first course, remove the strings.

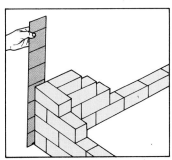

Proceed to build up several courses at each end of the wall,

using a gauge rod to keep each one to the correct height.

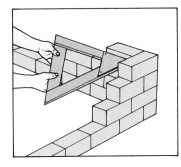

If the wall is to turn a corner, check with a builder's square that the courses are at 90 degrees.

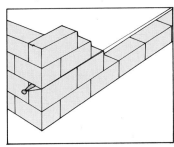

Use line pins with string stretched between them to keep the courses level between the ends. Move the line up one course as you finish each one.

Check occasionally with a spirit level that the sides are

vertical and that the courses are running straight.

Rake out the excess mortar from the joints to a depth of about 12mm every few courses to leave them open for pointing.

Pointing

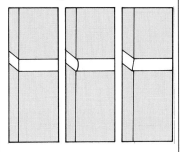

There are three shapes of joints: *flush, concave* and *weather-struck.*

Each starts with using a pointing trowel to push a sausage of mortar into the joint. Hold the mortar board just underneath the joint to catch any mortar that falls.

Make a *flush* joint by trimming off the excess mortar with the trowel and rubbing the remainder flush with a piece of rough cloth or sacking.

A *concave* joint is produced by pulling a rounded stick or the end of a cut length of hose along the joint to remove the excess mortar.

Use the trowel or a roller pointing tool to make a *weather-struck* joint.

Press the edge of the trowel into the joint to slope the mortar downwards and outwards until it slightly overhangs the brick below. Vertical joints are sloped from one side toward the other.

GATES

A gate marks the entrance to your home and garden and tells the passer-by a lot about you and your priorities. It can be welcoming or warning; it can offer security, privacy and decoration.

In selecting the right gate for your fence or wall, you should consider how serious you are about keeping animals in or out or your children off the road; whether it will be locked to keep intruders out, or is merely a way through the 'barrier' you have built to protect your family and property.

When you have decided what functions you want the gate to serve there are lots of styles and materials to choose from.

Where possible you should try to select a style which is in keeping with the house. For instance, a country cottage will probably look better with a simple wooden gate, whereas a Victorian town house would look better with a decorative wrought iron design.

Gates can be features in themselves – brightly painted, ornamental in design, or made from imaginative and unusual materials. Or they can be used to emphasize some other visual characteristic: to frame a view or underline a transition from one 'world' to another.

Above *These wooden garden gates are just two of the many designs available. They have been hung on concrete posts.*

Left *The design and proportions of this fence and gate exactly fit the space available. A small seat has been incorporated to add further interest.*

Top *A tall wooden gate with panels of trellis inset is ideal for an entrance on to a busy road.*

Above *A painted picket gate with fence to match, attractive but not too intrusive. A suitable style of fence for small town houses or country cottages.*

Left *A wrought iron gate on brick pillars, topped with urns, makes an impressive entrance to this leafy garden.*

25

Fitting Gates

There are few things more annoying than a gate that does not close properly. While fences and walls are required only to stand up, gates are expected to open and close year in and year out. People bang them open and shut, children swing on them and the elements do their best to ruin them.

There are three main causes of problems with gates. The most common one is the post on which it is hung. Even lightweight gates can cause a post to lean inwards. At first this causes the latch to misalign, so the gate will not stay closed. Eventually the gap between the posts is too small for the gate to close at all. The way to prevent this is to ensure the gateposts are set securely and can easily support the weight of the gate.

The second cause of trouble is hardware. Hinges and latches can fail through corrosion (or perhaps from not being up to the job in first place) but usually it is the screws or bolts that hold them on that cause the trouble. It is important to use strong fixings and also to check them occasionally to prevent them from coming loose.

The last cause of problems is the structure of the gate. As the entire weight of the gate is supported on one side only, there is a strong tendency for it to sag. This is overcome in most types of gate by a diagonal brace running from the top corner of the latch side to the bottom one on the hinge side. If the wood or metal deteriorates through rot or rust to the point that it begins to sag, it must either be completely rebuilt or replaced.

Types of gate

There are so many different styles of gate produced that it makes sense to use ready-made ones rather than make them yourself.

Vertical and horizontal close-boarded gates look similar to the ready-made fence panels, but have a more substantial frame and diagonal bracing to prevent sagging.

Frame and panel gates can look simple and rural or formal and grand. Hardwood gates can complement all types of fence and wall.

Barred gates make an attractive entrance to a drive. They come in pairs or as a single wide gate, sometimes with a smaller gate for pedestrians at the latch side. The wide gates need substantial posts, securely set in concrete.

Wrought iron gates are made in many designs and often have hinges and latches already fitted.

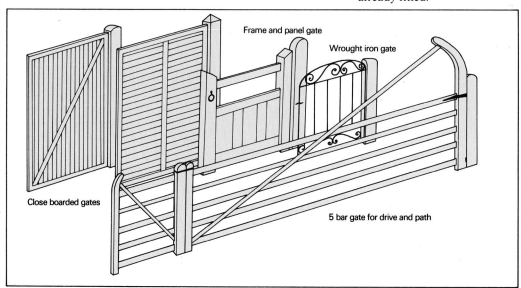

Frame and panel gate

Wrought iron gate

Close boarded gates

5 bar gate for drive and path

Hinges and latches

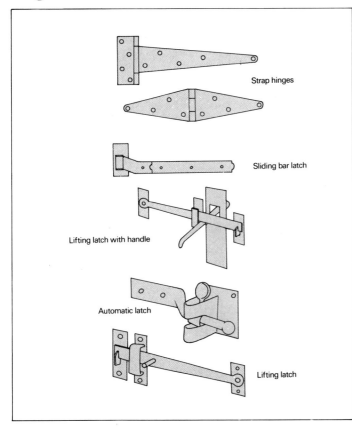

Strap hinges

Sliding bar latch

Lifting latch with handle

Automatic latch

Lifting latch

hang in the centre of the posts and to open in both directions if desired. The gate can also be hung overlapping the inside of the posts.

Both wooden and metal gates can be hung on pin-and-socket hinges. These allow the gate to be lifted off and to open in both directions. Hinge pins are made with various devices to fix them to posts or walls.

Simple latches such as the hook and staple and sliding bar and bolt must be operated each time the gate is opened or closed. Automatic latches are opened by hand, but allow the gate to be closed by simply pushing shut.

Hanging gates

Gates are easily hung, provided the space between posts or wall opening is regular in shape and the right size.

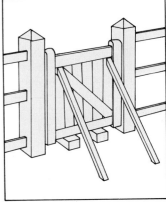

Strap hinges are used for wooden gates. They have holes through which to screw or bolt the straps to the post and the horizontal rails of the gate.

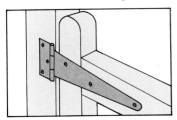

The simplest ones hold the gate flush with one side of the posts.

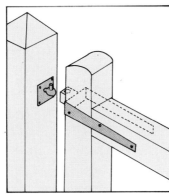

More sophisticated double strap hinges allow the gate to

Prop the gate in the opening at a height that will allow it to clear the ground by 50mm at its highest point. Hold the hinge and latch fittings up to check that there is sufficient clearance at the sides.

Then attach the hinges to both post (or wall) and gate.

MAINTENANCE

The autumn is the best time to undertake regular maintenance, when plants are dying down and there is more space for manoeuvre.

All timber fences will rot in time, so it is important to treat them regularly with wood preservative.

Walls will need pointing from time to time, in order to preserve their weatherproofing.

Painted surfaces that are subject to weather deteriorate very quickly and need regular maintenance. Before painting your fence or wall for the first time, ask yourself if you are willing to repaint every year or so. All exterior paintwork should be inspected and if necessary repainted.

When possible do exterior painting in late summer, following a dry spell. If it has to be done during bad weather, always wipe the woodwork dry and work on the sunny side of the house first.

Pointing

The mortar between bricks is called pointing. It sometimes needs replacing to preserve weather resistance.

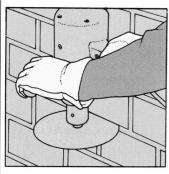

Fit a masonry-cutting disc to your power drill to remove

the old mortar. Brush the joints well to remove any loose mortar.

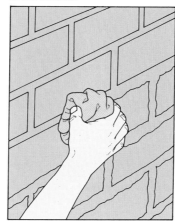

Fill the joints with new mortar, pressing in firmly to make sure there are no air bubbles. Try to wipe off any excess, which will look unsightly when dry.

Repairing Wooden Posts

Wooden posts need repair when they rot below ground level. The best means of repair is a concrete spur.

Saw through the post just above ground level. It will be necessary to remove any gravel boards to do this.

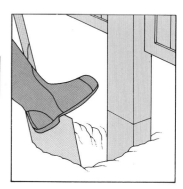

Dig out the remainder of the post from the side where the spur will be fitted. Continue digging to a depth of half the height of the post above ground. Make sure you have removed all decayed wood and loose soil from the hole.

Ram hard core into the bottom of the hole.

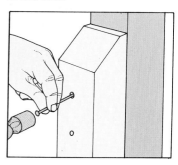

Prop the spur so that about 150mm projects into the hole

and mark the post through the holes in the spur. Remove the spur and drill the holes through the post.

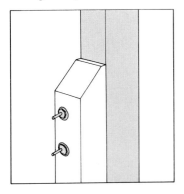

Replace the spur and bolt it securely to the post with galvanised coach bolts. The bolt heads should be on the face of the post and the washers and nuts should be on the spur side. Raise the post and spur if necessary to make the fence level and prop the spur with a rock or brick beneath. A few blows on the top of the post with a mallet will make sure the support is solid.

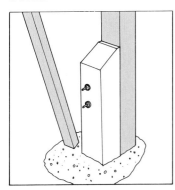

A simple pair of braces will hold the post vertical.
  Pack the hole with concrete,

ramming it down to fill any gaps. Finish the top by sloping it toward the edges to encourage water to run off.
  Concrete is also a cure for a leaning post.
  If an entire post needs replacing you will have to remove the fence from the post as gently as possible.

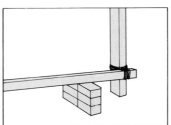

Use a post as a lever to pull the defective one from the ground. Then set the new one as described in 'Erecting fences' (page 11).

Arris Rails

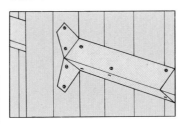

Broken arris rails on vertical boarded fences can be repaired with metal angle brackets made for the purpose.

Tip
When hanging a pair of gates, use G-clamps to hold them together as one piece. Use a packing strip between the meeting stiles to ensure the correct clearance.

Gateposts

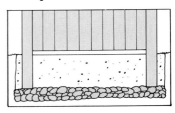

A pair of gateposts that refuse to remain stable can cause the gate to be out of line. They can be supported by tying them together below ground level.

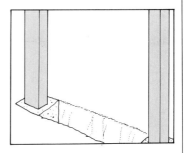

Remove the turf or paving between the posts and dig a trench as wide and deep as the post holes. Brush the soil from the concrete plugs and consolidate the soil in the floor of the trench.

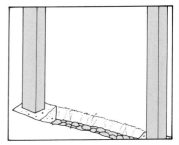

Ram a layer of hardcore into the trench and fill with fresh concrete up to the level required to support the turf or paving.

TRELLIS

Top *Raised brick beds and trellis fixed to the walls give maximum space for plants in this tiny patio garden. The white painted walls reflect the sun.*

Above *A rough wood trellis has been erected to separate the vegetable and flower garden.*

Left *To achieve an ambitious design of trellis like the one in this city garden you would need to order the material from a decorative trellis supplier. You could, however, produce a less ambitious version with ready-made panels of various sizes.*